ABYSMAL DOWNPOUR

A COLLECTION OF LIMERICKS

SWARNIKA

ISBN 979-888569155-0

Humor isn't Error

Error is Humor

Contents

Preface *ix*

Acknowledgements *xi*

Swarnika

1. The Book That Fell 5
2. Painted With Love 6
3. A Vile Of Smile 7
4. Building Heights 8
5. Crushed Like Paper 9

Putul Mangni Mandal

6. Cooking Rice 15
7. Many A Time 16
8. Slapped 17
9. Shut In 18
10. The Plight Of The Keys 19

Gauri Shukla

11. Ducked Hen 23
12. Buttered With Love 24
13. The School Choir 25
14. Shall We Vote? 26
15. Glassed Vision 27

Khushi Kaushik

16. Bloody Night 31
17. Mosquito's Kiss 32
18. Fairly Ugly 33

Contents

19. Bitter Honey 34

20. Lazy Winters 35

Raman Singh

21. Oven 39

22. Limerick 40

23. Stung 41

24. Cold Drink 42

25. The Last Verse 43

Deepanshi Ailawadi

26. Memories 47

27. Day And Night 48

28. Newspaper 49

29. Her Destination 50

30. Wounds 51

Nishtha Trehan

31. Five-second Rule 55

32. Slipped 56

33. Bumblebee 57

34. Night's Scare 58

35. Another Cookie 59

Hoilalnei Hmar

36. Was That You Pam? 63

37. She Bought Meat 64

38. 8god8 65

Contents

39. Doctor's Break 66

40. Heavenly Abode 67

Thank You! 69

Preface

Abysmal Downpour is a collection of poetry that has been uniquely designed. The collection is the result of a project taken up by Nrityangana Kala Kendra where each poet had to submit five poems each. Each of these poems, just like a limerick, had to be five lines long with a rhyming scheme of AABBA. There are forty poems in this collection written by eight poets. The poems range from sarcastic limericks to nonsensical puns. While the collection doesn't strictly follow the metrical retribution of a limerick, it follows the rhyming scheme and has a pinch of humor added to it.

Acknowledgements

Working on this collection has been a wonderful experience, but it wouldn't have been the same without the dedication and contributions made by my fellow poets. All of them have written beautifully and they've exhibited initiative as well as pertinence.

I'd like to thank Gauri Shukla, Khushi Kaushik, Putul Mangni Mandal, Raman Singh, Deepanshi Ailawadi, Nishtha Trehan, and Hoilalnei Hmar for working on the poetry present in this book and sharing them with our readers.

Swarnika

Swarnika is an avid reader and an ambivert. She is a glass-half-full kind of a person, not because she is always an optimist but because she believes that a glass that is full has no more scope and ends up creating the most amount of spills.

She completed her Bachelor's and Master's degree from the University of Delhi. She has completed her three-level professional certification in Spanish from Valencia Polytechnic University, Spain. She has also completed her certificate program in French from St. Stephen's College, University of Delhi. She is currently pursuing a Post-Graduate Diploma in Business Administration from Symbiosis Centre for Distance Learning, Pune. She is working on her thesis and research papers to earn her Ph.D. degree in English Literature.

She has a keen interest in criminology and detective fiction. Writings that indulge mystery and rationale speak volumes to her. She has earned her TEFL and TESOL certificates as an English language teacher. She is also a certified dance teacher with specializations in Bharatnatyam, Kathak, and Contemporary. She is also certified in Classical Music and Fine Arts.

She exhibits abundant admiration for food and would call herself a foodie. She believes in living in the moment rather than giving the moment the opportunity to live through you without you even realizing it. She has started her company- Nrityangana Kala Kendra OPC Private Limited on her own. She has been tutoring kids along with mentoring graduate and postgraduate students in academic and creative writing.

On some days she is a dreamer while on others she is a realist. She firmly believes in humanism. Nature mesmerizes her. On a usual day, you'd find her curled up in a corner either with a book or watching a movie/episode while relishing food.

She has initiated this project and has edited the book along with compiling it.

1. The Book That Fell

I opened a book and it fell;
It had a story that it wouldn't tell.
"I fell in front of thee,
Before you fall for me"
A faint voice dispersed with the sound of the knell.

- Swarnika

2. Painted With Love

I had a word with my paintbrush;
I was informed that it had a crush.
Embracing the canvas sheet,
The bristles throbbed when they meet
And Painted the musical notes of a thrush.

- Swarnika

3. A Vile Of Smile

No one knows how precious is the smile
Or they'd smile more than once in a while;
They who run after wealth,
Always smiling and in health;
Or perhaps they'll sell them in a vile.

- Swarnika

4. Building Heights

Mary Jane looked up at the sky,
Towering buildings racing high.
Who are they competing with?
Is the speed their pith?
The destination is achieved by nigh...

- Swarnika

5. Crushed Like Paper

Crushing a piece of paper today
She asked to bring it back to the bay.
"Just like it can't be plain again,
Your apologies are in vain."
A new sheet in hand, he said "don't stay".

- Swarnika

Putul Mangni Mandal

Living in New Delhi, Putul Mangni Mandal was born in December 1996. It is a pseudonym that she has adopted for the literary world. By root, her family comes from Bihar and as mentioned in the name, she belongs to the Mandal community. However, she abhors rigid statism or communism. Putul (meaning doll; it is her mother's pet name) lives with her small family of four. Financially, she is lower middle class. She studied in a government school named Sarvodaya Co. Ed. Senior Secondary in Nanak Pura. She has done her Post Graduation in English from Delhi University and aspires to become a professional writer, too, among many other possible-impossible things.

Poems have fascinated her ever since she read Kanyadān, a poem by the famous romantic Hindi writer Suryakānt Tripāthi 'Nirālā' in tenth grade. But she never knew that she could write until the day when her teacher Minākshi Mehta asked the whole class to create something. She composed her first poem Lakshya. Since then she has written many poems. Some of her English poems include On a Bus, Chores, Substitute, My Days, At Last, A Signal, and many others. She also writes in Hindi/Urdu and some of them are Intezār, Ūpar-Neechey, Bheetar, Chāl, etc. Fingers crossed, she hopes to soon come up with her poem collection. Not limiting herself to poems only, she has initiated in the field of prose writing through her first work Listen Didi which is a novella. Apart from this she also likes to write articles and essays on various literary topics.

She hopes that people will find something interesting and unique in her work. If they do so, they may use her email address given below to express their useful views.

Putulmangnimandal@gmail.com

6. Cooking Rice

Maa had told me the method twice
She said: warm it... low flame... And spice?
Oh, I had forgotten her process of cooking
So had to suffer a few failures through practicing
Now I, in my own new methods, cook separate rice!

- Putul Mangni Mandal

7. Many A Time

Many a time my heart was broken
Many a time it would have spoken
Many a time it prefers not to believe
Many a time it wishes to be lost in sleep
But by every new morning, it is awoken.

– Putul Mangni Mandal

8. Slapped

"Oh, I bet! anybody else would've lost his brain
But I believe that you can laugh even in such pain
Well I'm impressed coz' you're the most brave
Let me see your strength once more, I do crave"
If says a politician lifting to slap, would you refrain?

- Putul Mangni Mandal

9. Shut In

Vultures are whirling in the gray sky
Like over the stagnant water floats a fly
And they ask: Take a look at this ugly world,
Please stay behind the door for it's absurd!
But sitting inside, how can I let life pass by.

- Putul Mangni Mandal

10. The Plight Of The Keys

What did that innocent keypad do to you?
You scrawny long fingers, don't you have a clue?
You beat them and you beat all day long
You slave it and say: "only to me it belongs".
Like you take a break, your phone needs too!

- Putul Mangni Mandal

Gauri Shukla

Gauri Shukla is a third-year Literature student pursuing her passion for reading and writing from the University of Delhi. President of the Literary Society of the college, she is an avid reader who yearns to get lost in estranged, galvanic worlds of art. A national-level debater, she is someone who doesn't shy away from speaking her mind. An ardent scripturient, she has written articles for The Times of India, The Hindu, The Redstockings Chronicles, etc. She's currently working on a South-Asian anthology as an editor alongside editors from Bangladesh and Pakistan. Her main interests of study lie in Diasporic postcolonial and African-American literature. She wishes to document the experiences and sentiments of different people, belonging to different cultures, all around the world. She believes life is too short and time is fleeting thus, each moment needs to be savored and felt to its optimum level. She likes to describe herself as a wandering cloud that romances with the sky, lost yet free.

11. Ducked Hen

The duck chased the hen
Straight out of its pen.
Wobbling on its webbed feet,
It trotted behind the hen looking neat
As if chasing the hen was its zen.

- Gauri Shukla

12. Buttered With Love

Once upon a time, there was a man who loved butter;
All day and night, he saw nothing but butter
So, when he got stranded on an island
He became frantic like a miner who loses his diamond
Without butter, his body shut down like a shop's shutter.

- Gauri Shukla

13. The School Choir

The song went up and down the scales
As the students sang like whales.
With fleeting voices sounding like those of a siren,
The children looked like rabbits from a warren
Leaving behind melodious trails.

- Gauri Shukla

14. Shall We Vote?

The women went achoo, achoo!
The men went boo hoo, boo hoo!
The procession looked like a sticky orange fluid,
Slowly making its way through the crowd seemingly languid
As people around guffawed at the politician's gobbledygoo.

- Gauri Shukla

15. Glassed Vision

She took off her glasses
To look cool in her high school classes.
But because she could hardly see,
She did not see that she was the only odd tree
Since half of the students wore glasses.

- Gauri Shukla

Khushi Kaushik

Khushi Kaushik, the elder child in a nuclear family, was born and brought up in Faridabad, Haryana. She studied in DAV public school, sec 14, Faridabad, and was good in studies since childhood. She had a keen interest in studying literature. The author of 'Secret of room 333' is known for her flash fiction. She started writing her first book when she was 13, which is a very young age , her interest developed in the field of content writing and she started to write poems , stories and finally decided to write a fiction . She is 20 at present and is pursuing English literature from University of Delhi. Apart from being an author she is a poetess as well and her compilation of romantic poems 'Shades of love' had a great readership. She is an eager learner and has various interests. She has a keen interest in art, she has been painting since childhood and is a very good singer as well and also has won competitions in singing . She has a dynamic personality and is someone who loves to take up new challenges and broaden her horizons.

16. Bloody Night

Once upon a time a Knight
Who walked in the dark night.
He stepped on something chubby,
And it was also too clumsily shabby.
He saw his baby when he turned on the light.

- Khushi Kaushik

17. Mosquito's Kiss

There was once a mosquito,
That was sitting on the mistletoe.
The blinds came to kiss
But mistaken they miss,
Kissed the little mosquito.

- Khushi Kaushik

18. Fairly Ugly

Nanny was a girl who was fair
She ran and fell then was in fear
She broke her arm
Her face was in harm
Now ugly she was no one came near.

- Khushi Kaushik

19. Bitter Honey

Brode had a witty sister
Her tone was naturally bitter
With all her money
If she bought honey
Then she'd make the honey too bitter.

– Khushi Kaushik

20. Lazy Winters

We say we love a wintery day
When we all stay in bed and lay
Because then we have an excuse
Not to work and refuse
As we all are lazy but we just don't say.

- Khushi Kaushik

Raman Singh

Raman Singh was born in the year 2001 in Haryana, India. He never did things to pass time, when he held on to a thing, he gave himself completely to it. May it be playing basketball for nine years, may it be doing theatre, which also induced interest in literature. He is currently pursuing BA(Hons) in English, from Delhi University, and is an important part of the theatre society. He has also acted in six theatrical productions and has written several short plays and stories. Not to forget his love for Hindi Literature, which has added new dimensions to his imaginations and in which he finds those values and thoughts which otherwise would've been too late to discover. If there is anything else that he loves, that is a cup of coffee. His notion of feeling content and happy is to have A cup of coffee with a brownie while reading a book.

21. Oven

A mother was crying for his lost boy named Oven.
People came and with pity asked, "Oh! When?"
We went on a Christmas fest.
He sat down for a while to rest.
And her mother started to cry again "Oven! Oven! Oven!"

- Raman Singh

22. Limerick

In a limerick you need to write nonsense
It doesn't demand to make any sense
First, choose a topic which is trivial
Which should lack any kind of potential
Now pick up the pen and write without being tense.

- Raman Singh

23. Stung

"Doctor my heart bleeds with an attack of Javelin
Please wipe this blood with a napkin and give me an aspirin"
You should go home and rest
That would be best
"No, rather give me masculine for I have been stung by a feminine."

- Raman Singh

24. Cold Drink

I ordered a cold drink
They give me a black drink
I asked them to change this
They looked at me like I was a whiz
What they gave me now was green, to the brink but still not my COLD drink.

- Raman Singh

25. The Last Verse

It is the last one I am writing
There will be no more of rhyming
I have to think so much
My mind has to rush
This is the last line and now I am chilling.

- Raman Singh

Deepanshi Ailawadi

Deepanshi Ailawadi holds a Master's degree in English Literature. Since childhood libraries are her second home which enables her to travel across time and space. She believes each written page tells a story that should not be left unheard because in the end human beings are made up of little stories stored up in their brain's memory. Writing is one of the mediums through which stories can be heard, touched, and felt. Thus, she decided to write, to pay back her debt to Reading and disseminate stories that have the capability to reform our ways of perception. Writing enables her to hold several personalities and perspectives in her body, sometimes she becomes a bookseller, while other times she becomes a buyer of the book, and sometimes she can be both her friend and her enemy at once. It is this magic that tempted her to write for others and for herself too.

26. Memories

Memories haunt when you disown
Them silently on the road unknown
Far from the known memories
Far from the heart's treasuries
They become aching cyclone.

- Deepanshi Ailawadi

27. Day and Night

Chilly and cold nights
In black sky fights for the white
Blissful and glowing day
While its spirit decay
And loses its blight.

- Deepanshi Ailawadi

28. Newspaper

Nowadays newspaper arrives my home
With petty cancel syndrome
Events, accidents and tragedies
Were sold in halfpennies
And buried beneath bright bureaucratic domes.

- Deepanshi Ailawadi

29. Her Destination

Women of different nations
Countries and continents have common destinations
To reach unfamiliar mirrors of light
Reflecting out of sight
Concealed, crumbled old foundations.

- Deepanshi Ailawadi

30. Wounds

Sometimes the wounds speak
After a long game of hide and seek
And recollect
Their long lost affect
By breaking the body with a creak.

– Deepanshi Ailawadi

Nishtha Trehan

Nishtha Trehan is a student at Atma Ram Sanatan Dharma College, University of Delhi, studying English Honours. In her breaks, she likes to read, write, and journal. It is under the guidance of her supervisor, Swarnika, that she has been able to finish these poems.

31. Five-Second Rule

Five-second rule
Works only for those few who drool
Others are way too engrossed
And are rather grossed
By the floor ice cream that's super cool.

- Nishtha Trehan

32. Slipped

On a slope so slippy
My dad screamed hippie
Watching my mom fall
Cue the silenced drawl
An hour later dad is weepy.

– Nishtha Trehan

33. Bumblebee

Hickety pickety bumblebee
The point of this life I see
Is to live, not just exist
So you must continue to persist
Everyone get this, you hear me?

– Nishtha Trehan

34. Night's Scare

I met a ghost last night.
He told me your plight-
Said you had trouble lying asleep,
That has him worried deep.
Hurry up, he yearns for your fright.

- Nishtha Trehan

35. Another Cookie

"Just one more?"
For another cookie, I implore
Relenting, my mother doesn't disagree
She doesn't know later I'll take another and flee
WOHOO! YES! GOD, YES! I SWORE.

- Nishtha Trehan

Hoilalnei Hmar

Hoilalnei Hmar is a college student from Rajdhani College, Delhi University. Currently residing in Manipur, she is a feminist. Not to mention, she had a very interesting life in high school where she graduated from Christ Jyoti School, Mantripukhri (Imphal). She worked on herself and evolved herself as a better person when she attended Don Bosco Higher Secondary School, Maram(Manipur).

36. Was That You Pam?

Pam was alone when she farted
After her friends and she parted
The noise of thunder heard from afar
Because the sound was from the bar
And she acted like she never farted.

- Hoilalnei Hmar

37. She Bought Meat

As Selly was walking down the street
She fell on the sand under the heat
Not knowing where to go
And feeling shy about it so
She bought a whole package of meat.

- Hoilalnei Hmar

38. 8God8

Eight is infinity
God is divinity
Devil is weak
When you are a freak
For he is in every vicinity.

– Hoilalnei Hmar

39. Doctor's Break

An apple a day keeps the doctor away
But what will keep them away for a day?
It is something that makes us curious
But loaded work keeps them furious
Think of the solution until your hair turn grey.

- Hoilalnei Hmar

40. Heavenly Abode

Heaven is a place
Where a fairy will be your face
Where you will be free
Under the tree
But be careful with your pace.

- Hoilalnei Hmar

Thank You!

Dear Reader,

I'd like to thank you for reading our collection of limericks. I really hope you could appreciate the work done by all the poets in Abysmal Downpour. If you'd like to reach us, you can send us an email at Swara@nrityanganakalakendra.com. Your feedback is valued.

Regards,

Swarnika

9 798885 691550

Printed by Libri Plureos GmbH in Hamburg, Germany